MIGHTY MACHINES

A LEGO® ADVENTURE IN THE REAL WORLD

All aboard for a monster machine adventure!

▟ SCHOLASTIC

New York   Toronto   London   Auckland
Sydney   Mexico City   New Delhi   Hong Kong

Welcome, LEGO fans!

LEGO® minifigures show you the world in a unique nonfiction program.

This leveled reader is part of a program of LEGO® nonfiction books, with something for all the family, at every age and stage. LEGO nonfiction books have amazing facts, beautiful real-world photos, and minifigures everywhere, leading the fun and discovery.

To find out more about the books in the program, visit www.scholastic.com.

Leveled readers from Scholastic are designed to support your child's efforts to learn how to read at every age and stage.

LEVEL 1 READER

Beginning reader
Preschool–Grade 1
Sight words
Words to sound out
Simple sentences

LEVEL 2 READER

Developing reader
Grades 1–2
New vocabulary
Longer sentences

LEVEL 3 READER

Growing reader
Grades 1–3
Reading for inspiration and information

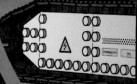

BUILD IT!

Check out the epic building ideas when you see me.

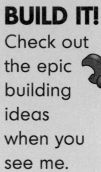

If you see a word in **bold**, you can find out what it means on page 31.

Hey, can I have a lift? I need to get to the end of this book!

7632

Look around you. Machines help out everywhere! Giant diggers lift tons of dirt. Long trains pull cars full of people. Rockets blast into space.

Mighty machines are super strong . . . just like me!

I wonder how much the biggest digger bucket can hold?

It's big enough to scoop me! I'm off!

Start your engines.
Let's go!

BUILD IT!
Build your own mighty machine. Will it have wheels or wings?

Make way! Longest road train coming through!

Let's build a road! Call in the digger. The digger has an arm called a boom. It has a bucket on the end. The sharp teeth **scoop** out dirt.

The biggest digger in the world could hold 4,000 soccer balls.

Awesome! I'll kick them in. GOAL!

The biggest diggers are as heavy as 400 cars!

BUILD IT!
Build a digger. How many LEGO bricks can you scoop up?

The dump truck brings dirt and rocks to make the road. It may hold about 25 tons of dirt.

The biggest dump truck tire is as tall as 100 minifigures!

That's as heavy as 5 big elephants! It tips out the dirt ready for the bulldozers.

Call in the bulldozer! The bulldozer uses a big **blade** to push the dirt and rocks. It makes everything flat. A super dozer has a blade that is as wide as 462 minifigures!

Our road needs to go through that old building.

Stand back! I'm going to blow the building up.

Oops. Wrong one! Quick, where's the bulldozer?

The bulldozer has giant tracks to help it move. I'd better make tracks!

Bring in the steamroller!
It may weigh 20 tons.
It smoothes **asphalt**
onto the road.
Now the road is built.
Let's drive!

Help! I don't want to become a flatbread!

Chill out, man. It's only traveling at 2 miles per hour!

BUILD IT!

Build cars, motorcyles, and trucks for your road. Create a huge traffic jam!

Concrete is good for building. The concrete mixer has a barrel that turns round and round. It mixes cement, rock, and water to make concrete. When the concrete is poured out, it hardens.

Ooh, I'm sinking into this concrete.

Careful! Concrete turns hard really quickly.

Yikes! I'm not going to stick around to find out!

How do you build a super-tall building? A crane can lift what you need! The tallest crane can lift things up to 70 **stories** high.

BUILD IT!

Build a crane with a super-long arm. Remember to build a strong base for it!

I said pick up the bar, not my car!

Some machines are used to carry things. Honk honk! The road train is on its way. It can pull up to 100 **trailers**! Road trains are the longest trucks in the world.

Oh no, I think we've got a puncture.

Are you kidding me? There are 100s of tires to check.

Found it, finally! Yawn. That's tired me out . . .

BUILD IT!
Build a road train. How many trailers will it have?

Some trucks can carry other heavy things. A car transporter carries between 5 and 10 cars. The cars drive on and off **ramps**.

BUILD IT!

Build a car transporter to carry cars all around your house.

Heeeeave!

Cars weigh about 2 tons each! That's heavy.

All aboard! The **cargo** ship travels all over the world. It holds more than 2,000 big boxes. One ship may be as long as 13 blue whales!

Check this out! The biggest cargo ship can hold more than 745 million bananas!

Toot Toot! Trains pull cars full of people.

Can you tell me where the bathroom is please?

I'm afraid it's at the other end of the train.

Argh! This train is over half a mile long!

The longest trains have 44 cars.
One train in Japan travels at
375 mph!

Zoom! The Airbus jet flies at 540 mph. It holds more than 500 people.

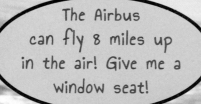

The Airbus can fly 8 miles up in the air! Give me a window seat!

It is the biggest plane in the world. It has two levels!

BUILD IT!

Build an awesome plane and take your minifigures on vacation.

AIRBUS A380-800

3, 2, 1, blast off! The Soyuz rocket blasts into space. It moves at 755 feet per second. It takes astronauts to a **space station**.

Look, aliens! But how did they get there?

We've got company. Let's get the flying saucer.

Hello there! Anyone up for a space race?

It's the mightiest machine of all!

BUILD IT!
Build a rocket to carry LEGO bricks into space. Perfect for building your space station!

Build a LEGO® construction site!

Mighty machines love to work. What will you build today?

Mighty machine words

asphalt
a black material that is used for making roads.

blade
the broad, flat part of a machine that pushes the material to be moved.

cargo
something that is carried from one place to another by a vehicle.

concrete
a hard, strong material that is used for building.

ramp
a slope that joins two surfaces of different heights.

scoop
to dig out.

space station
a large spacecraft in which people live, to do research and experiments.

story
a part of a building where all the rooms are on the same level—also called a "floor."

trailer
A wagon that carries heavy loads and is pulled by another vehicle.

This ax is no good. Bring in the mighty machines!

Shhh!

It's good to learn some mighty words!

Index

Credits

For the LEGO Group: Peter Moorby *Licensing Coordinator*; Heidi K. Jensen *Licensing Manager*;

Photos ©: cover main: Blaize Pascall/Alamy Images; cover top left: goce/iStockphoto; cover top right: Juanan Barros Moreno/Shutterstock, Inc.; cover, back cover tire tracks: Yevgen Solovyov/123RF; 1 cloudy sky and throughout: Pop Nukoonrat/Dreamstime; 1 main: Josie Elias/Getty Images; 2 center left: i-Stockr/iStockphoto; 2-3 bottom background: Bryljaev/Dreamstime; 4-5 train: John Kirk/iStockphoto; 6-7 main: gece33/iStockphoto; 7 top right: JamesYetMingAu-Photography/iStockphoto; 8-9 top: Maksym Dragunov/iStockphoto; 8 center left: Alasdair Thomson/iStockphoto; 10-11 main: Blaize Pascall/Alamy Images; 10-11 tape: Arcadia_dreamstime/Dreamstime; 11 center right: nulinukas/Shutterstock, Inc.; 12-13 background: mycola/iStockphoto; 12-13 main: Yudesign/Dreamstime; 13 bottom right: Molotok007/Dreamstime; 14-15: Krzyzak/Alamy Images; 16-17 top background: roman023/iStockphoto; 16 top: Lalocracio/iStockphoto; 17 top right: Various-Everythings/Shutterstock, Inc.; 18-19: Josie Elias/Getty Images; 20-21: Taina Sohlman/iStockphoto; 22-23: Peter Titmuss/Alamy Images; 24 bottom left: VCG/Getty Images; 24-25 main: Vincent St. Thomas/Shutterstock, Inc.; 26-27 background: Brian Kinney/Shutterstock, Inc.; 27 right: Artyom Anikeev/Shutterstock, Inc.; 28-29 background: olegkalina/iStockphoto; 28-29 main: NASA/Joel Kowsky/Alamy Images; 30-31 sky: Matthew Collingwood/Dreamstime; 30-31 bottom: Ciezkitemat/Dreamstime; 30 center left: keantian/Shutterstock, Inc.; 31 top left: gece33/iStockphoto.

All LEGO illustrations and stickers by Paul Lee and Sean Wang

Here are the LEGO bricks, ready for your next build!

ISBN 978-1-338-13020-1

10 9 8 7 6 5 4 3 2 1   16 17 18 19 20

Printed in the U.S.A.   40
First edition, March 2017